LAKE SUPERIOR *Secrets*

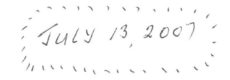

PHOTOGRAPHS & REFLECTIONS
BRUCE MONTAGNE

All inquiries should be addressed to:
   Ann Arbor Media Group LLC
   2500 S. State Street
   Ann Arbor, MI 48104

Printed and bound in Canada.

09 08 07 06 05   I   2   3   4   5

Library of Congress Cataloging-in-Publication Data

Montagne, Bruce, 1963-
  Lake Superior Secrets : photographs and reflections / Bruce Montagne.
    p. cm.
   ISBN-I3: 978-I-58726-293-7 (hardcover : alk. paper)
   ISBN-I0: I-58726-293-2 (hardcover : alk. paper)
  I. Superior, Lake—Pictorial works. 2. Superior, Lake—Description
and travel. 3. Superior, Lake, Region—Pictorial works. 4. Superior,
Lake, Region—Description and travel. I. Title.
  F552.M66 2005
   917.74'9'00222—dc22
                                     2005019819

ACKNOWLEDGMENTS

The creation of this book has not been a solitary pursuit.
My deep gratitude is extended to the following individuals:

Douglas Peterson for his infinite attention to detail
in both design and text editing which made this book a
reality and elevated it beyond mere words and images on
paper. Pulitzer prize winner **N. Scott Momaday** for his
excerpt and eloquent understanding of our bond with
the natural world.

Photographer **Gregory M. Nelson** for introducing me
to the common loon and accompanying me on several
Superior trips. Artist **Michael "Kyook" Monroe** who
brought laughter and friendship with him as we paddled
the shores of Isle Royale. Photographer **Claudia Adams**
who shared her secret shooting locations along Lake
Superior. Wildlife photographers **Carl R. Sams II** and
Jean Stoick for their steadfast encouragement. Nature
photographer **Ted Nelson** whose dedication to his self-
published book was a true inspiration.

Staff members at parks around the lake who offer
knowledge, helping us to learn, recreate, dream, and find
wonder in these special places. And all of the people on
my journeys who shared friendly conversation, a deep
connection with the lake, a warm cup of coffee, and
a heartfelt belief in this sometimes daunting project.

The excerpt on page 4 is from the book *The Way to
Rainy Mountain*, University of New Mexico Press, 1969,
by N. Scott Momaday, and is used with his permission.

Book Design: Douglas Alden Peterson, Visualeyes,
Brighton, MI

All wildlife appearing in this book was photographed in
the wild with the exception of the Canadian lynx, page
I47, which was under controlled conditions.

For
Donna and Donald Montagne
who ventured to a new country home
with their three young boys.
Within those hardwood forests,
shallow lakes, and critter-filled swamps,
I discovered the natural world
and my lifelong path.

*O*nce in his life a man
ought to concentrate his mind upon the remembered earth.
He ought to give himself up to a particular landscape in his
experience; to look at it from as many angles as he can,
to wonder upon it, to dwell upon it. He ought to imagine
that he touches it with his hands at every season and listens
to the sounds that are made upon it. He ought to imagine
the creatures there and all the faintest motions of the wind.
He ought to recollect the glare of the moon and the colors
of the dawn and dusk.

N. Scott Momaday

THE SECRETS

SILENCE 8

RHYTHMS 36

LIGHT 58

WHISPERS 86

POWER 104

FOOTPRINTS 118

DRAMA 134

*W*onder. I discovered it as a small boy in
southeastern Michigan, sitting quietly among giant oaks and maples, experiencing the natural rhythms
around me. Many years later, I coupled my passion for nature with a keen interest in photography.
An enticing magazine article about Pukaskwa National Park of Canada whetted my appetite
for the untamed and picturesque shores of Lake Superior.

When I first arrived at the lake, I was a blank canvas
and ready to absorb whatever this region offered me. What I found far exceeded my expectations.
I began exploring driftwood-littered beaches, ancient rocky headlands, and fragrant boreal forests.
I felt something unique lurked beneath the canopy of postcard beauty.

Stories yearned to be told here. The challenge was inviting
them into my lens. Intuition and serendipity became my guides. I slowed my pace and allowed events
to unfold before me. Faint scents would waft my way and I would follow. Small movements caught
my eye and led me to unexpected treasures.

By surrendering myself to the experience of exploring
on a sensual level, the true essence of the region began to reveal itself. Over the years, the realm
of Lake Superior moved from being one of just rock, sky, trees, and water to one much richer, more
complex and ethereal. Subtle themes and hidden worlds emerged. I discovered a place where intimate
scenes are as alluring as the grand vistas. Here, silence is loud, birch bark softly whispers, and
power is found in pebbles. These are the secrets of Lake Superior.

Dense fog quietly floats through a
motionless forest of black spruce
trees in Neys Provincial Park.

After the long drive north, I stopped at a secluded lake to stretch my legs and unwind. The rich, earthy aroma of early summer filled my nostrils as I took a deep breath. At the water's edge, I allowed the solitude to wash away the tensions of the drive. I closed my eyes and listened. Only natural sounds punctuated the tranquility.

Silence is a welcome companion here. It accentuates the subtle sounds around me. On that day, several warbler species whistled and sang. High in his spruce tree, a red squirrel belted out his unsettling chatter. Aspen leaves rustled in the breeze blowing across the lake. Small waves lapped against a few iron-stained rocks at my feet. First-time visitors, however, often find this quiet environment disconcerting. They are surprised how loud silence can be.

Silence discloses this region's true character. Under a deep veil of snow, winter transcends silence. The absence of sound is intensified by its contrast to your own deafening heartbeat. No birds sing. The squirrels are mute. In the brittle cold, any movement is arduous. Time is suspended. The black bear and chipmunk nestle in their dark, hidden sanctuaries. The land descends into a deep, slumbering sleep.

Though silence is most intense in winter, each season brings many forms of quiet stillness. It was mid-May and winter had finally released its grip. Life was unfolding around me. The first light of day revealed Marie Louise Lake through a dream-like fog. Sitting on a lichen-encrusted boulder, I immersed myself in the solitude. A single wolf suddenly howled through the curtain of mist. Like thousands of seasons before, the wolf and the silence clashed, each trying to overpower the other. In time, the howls faded.

The quiet returned with force following this battle. Yet the wolf's cry was not lost. It is etched in my memory. Whether it is the wind or the wolf or the warbler, the contender has no chance. Here, silence always wins.

The fog-enveloped shores of Marie Louise Lake at daybreak
conceal many secrets. Sleeping Giant Provincial Park

The warmth of spring slowly melts the
white of winter from a snowshoe hare.

A lone birch leaf rests in a dry channel of the Presque Isle River. Porcupine Mountains Wilderness State Park

In Lake Superior Provincial Park, an *Amanita muscaria* mushroom and rich autumn leaves compete for attention on the damp forest floor.

An early afternoon visit by the sandman inspires a silent yawn from this tranquil great gray owl.

Only the wind knows the destination of a flock of clouds as they race toward the distant horizon. Tettegouche State Park

Overleaf:
Winter transforms a hillside of young birches into a monochrome scene where deep snows hush the forest's sounds.

Over Lake Superior,
a ring-billed gull sails
effortlessly through
a sea of blue.

Hidden treasures lurk in a glassy pool on a barren island in Shot Watch Cove. Pukaskwa National Park

A crescent moon winks at the rising sun as dawn chases away the night sky in Moskey Basin. Isle Royale National Park

Tiny streams trickle down sandstone cliffs breaking the silence on a serene summer evening. Pictured Rocks National Lakeshore

A freezing slush batter creates pancake ice on a clear morning in this windless bay. Pukaskwa National Park

Thick layers of downy ice and snow muffle the rumble of Cascade Falls. Cascade River State Park

A palette of rich earth tones embellishes the bark of a mammoth
red pine in the Copper Country State Forest of Michigan.

Roaring waves have eroded the cliffs at Squaw Bay, but
on this day, they rest. Apostle Islands National Lakeshore

Overleaf:
The serenity of an early autumn morning is doubled
on a small moose pond in Pukaskwa National Park.

Soft morning sunlight dances on a trio of pink lady's slippers in Michigan's Superior National Forest.

A blanket of green
moss softens this
battle-scarred
boulder on a
fog-bound day.
Michipicoten Post
Provincial Park

The remains of a white-tailed buck reinforce the stillness of winter on snow-covered dunes in the Apostle Islands.

In Lake Superior
Provincial Park, a
crisp frost on maple
leaves and clover
foreshadows the
season of bitter cold.

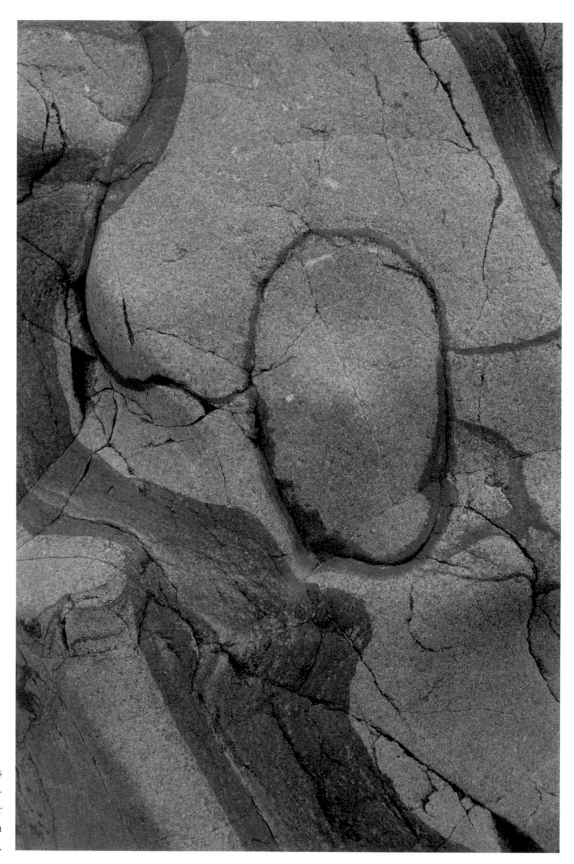

Whimsical patterns swirl through a wave-polished boulder along Agate Beach near Copper Harbor.

Superior provides wondrous gifts on this Christmas morning. Cold and steam unite to frost a lone birch tree along a beach strewn with boulders in Old Woman Bay. Lake Superior Provincial Park

Side by side, the Sleeping Giant and Superior rest peacefully this crisp dawn.
The lake snuggles under a blanket of fog. Sleeping Giant Provincial Park

Cobblestones watch as storm clouds build
over Oiseau Bay. Pukaskwa National Park

The shell of a white-tailed buck fuses with
the sand along the shoreline of Sand Point.
Pictured Rocks National Lakeshore

hythms pulse through this living landscape. Clocks and calendars become trivial; minutes, weeks, and years are meaningless. Superior Time governs here. Seasons gradually change and natural wonders evolve. While the pace of life in populated areas far beyond the horizon pounds, this remote area lumbers but never falters.

The rhythmic beat is defined in the transitions. Snows fade only when warmth prevails and tints the trees in lime. Ferns unfurl. New generations arrive. Bees pollinate the cornucopia of wildflowers. Life triumphs. Then, slowly, the forests quiet and leaves rim with frost. Bathed in warm tones, birch and maple compete for attention. Wind rakes the trees revealing their stark, bony architecture. The naked earth soon nestles under a thick, white blanket until warm breezes journey north to wake it again. Solstice and equinox are mere guidelines. Each season solemnly enters, leaves its mark, then reluctantly moves on its way.

Large and small, visible and hidden, other rhythms flow within these transitions. Waves of avian migrants ebb and flow like tides. The beach sand consumes a deer abandoned by the coyote and raven. The elements frolic and visual rhythms emerge. Frigid air weaves lace in blue ice. Wind sculpts white ripples in snow. Lichen, fueled by the sun, inches over terraced cobblestones. Patterns. Colors. Sounds. Odors. Each element contributes its part to the pulse.

A tiny nook along a river becomes the final resting place for a pink salmon. The current has shrouded it in autumn maple leaves. Each element within this tableau is perfectly composed to fittingly honor the end of a life. Tomorrow the colors will begin to fade. Following the winter snows, the spring thaw will wash away every trace of this moment except the image in this book. On the cliff above, a red squirrel with a mouthful of seeds scurries to stock its winter nest in the trunk of a grand white pine. Finales are followed by preludes. Here, it is an incessant, rhythmic unfolding.

Strands of ice form harmonious patterns on a cliff west of Sand Point. Apostle Islands National Lakeshore

By the time Michigan's Big Iron River carves through this natural rock dam, many more autumns will reflect in its pools.

Unique in shape but similar in color, wave-tumbled cobblestones huddle in a quiet corner along Perry Bay. Sleeping Giant Provincial Park

Superior sleeps under a blanket of lacy ice. Gooseberry Falls State Park

Timid ferns are lured out in May by the warm touch of morning sunlight.

Driven by late November winds, a silent migration of clouds travel southward over the Grand Sable Dunes. Pictured Rocks National Lakeshore

Unaware of the challenges ahead, the early days of red fox pups are consumed by frolic, exploration, and devoted attention from mom. Becoming solitary by autumn, they will wander the forests seeking territories of their own.

Overleaf:
Vivid autumn leaves
find refuge in an
alcove of steel-gray
slate along the
Big Iron River.

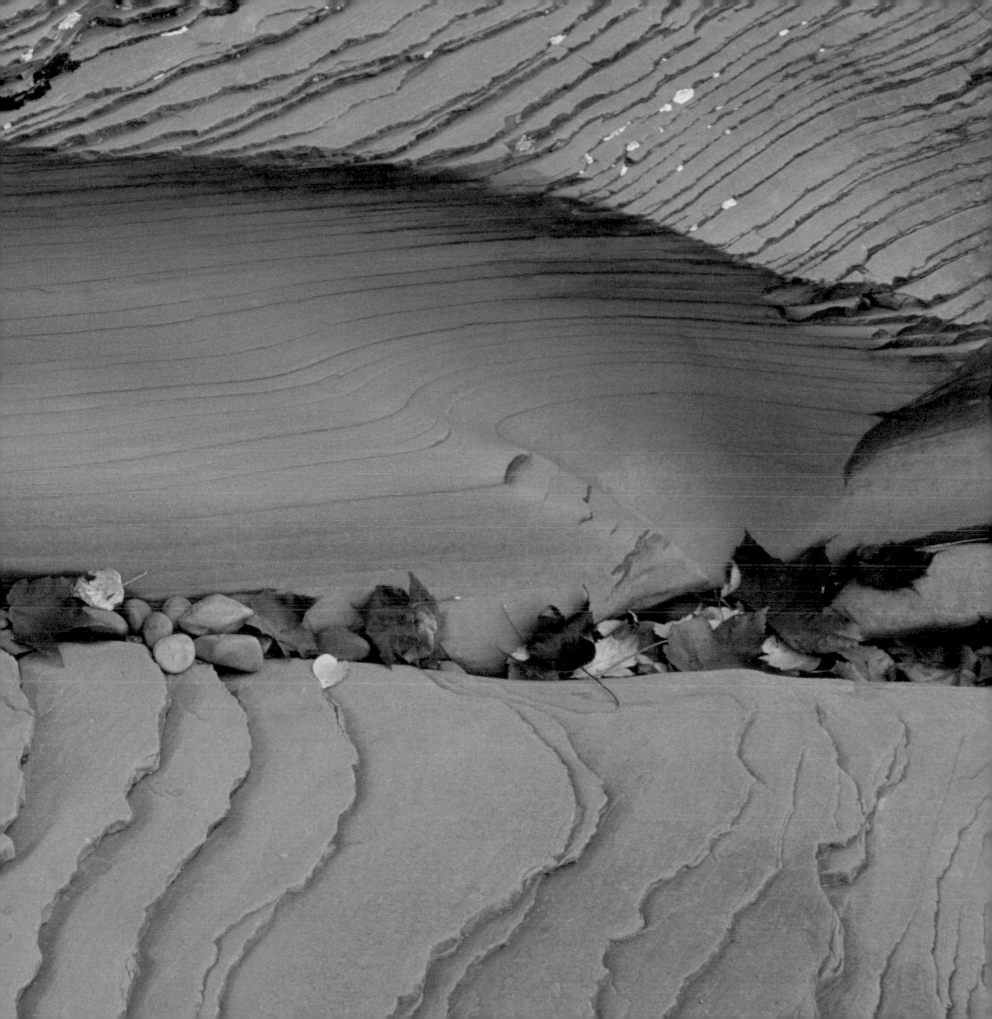

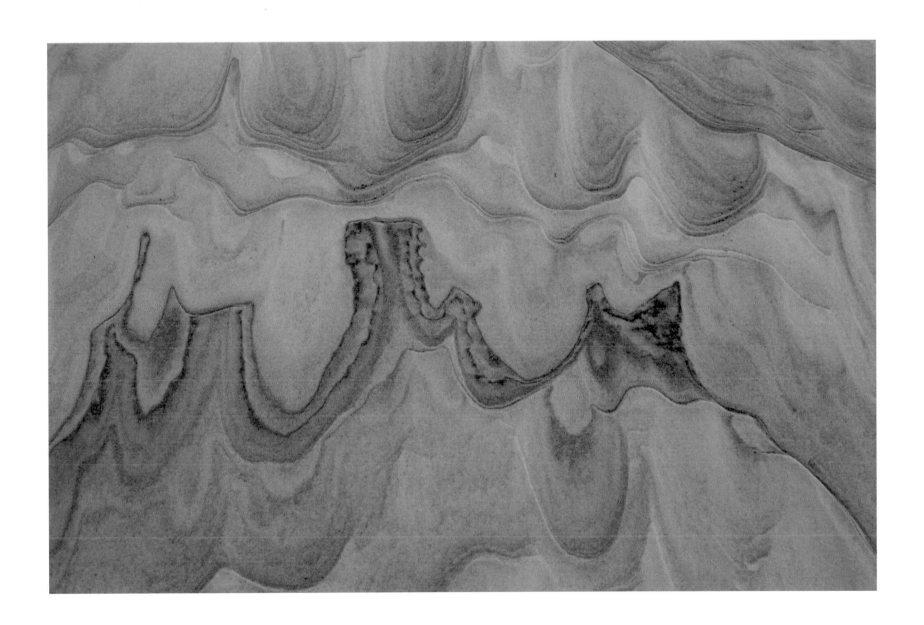

Brilliant fallen leaves become a fitting tribute
to a pink salmon whose colors fade at death.

Wind paints its moods with sand and snow along the
Pic River Dunes in mid-winter. Pukaskwa National Park

Ribbons of light
and shadow mingle
on the windswept
snows of Perry Bay.
Sleeping Giant
Provincial Park

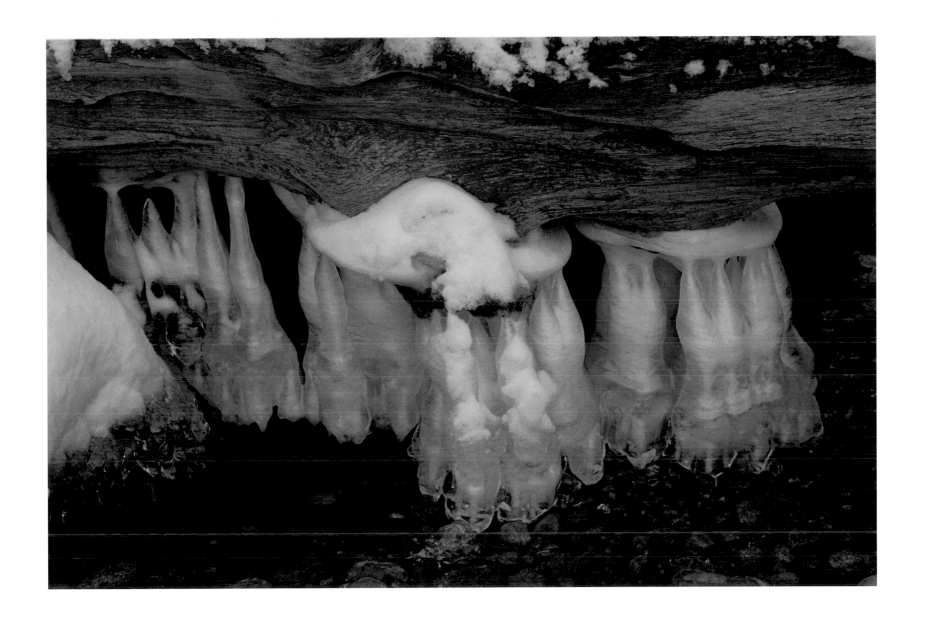

Winter drapes icy pillars from a weathered log
into a shallow pool. Chippewa River, Ontario

Overleaf:
On the exposed tip of Michigan's Whitefish Point, water, sand,
and pebbles continually find new ways to amuse themselves.

Spring arrives, bathing the Kama Hills in
gentle green after many months of stark white.

Ripples of sand are the only waves that are found this
day in a tranquil cove. Michipicoten Post Provincial Park

A marooned
chandelier from a
distant forest now
points due west as
the sun sets at the
Pic River Dunes.
Pukaskwa
National Park

Patterns continually change as tiny bubbles parade in a tannin-stained eddy. Lake Superior Provincial Park

Dawn struggles as frigid temperatures transform the lake's steam into a dense blanket that hugs the surface in late December. Split Rock Lighthouse State Park

Warm. Cool. Lively. Raw. Soft. Raking. From sunup to sundown, the light in this northern wilderness holds magic. The fleeting hours near dawn and dusk are the most elegant. Shorelines blaze with rich oranges and auburns at daybreak. Glassy coves become gilded in gold. Shivering is momentarily stilled when winter landscapes are bathed in warm sunset pinks and mauves. Reflected clouds double as stepping-stones to the calm horizon as the sun is devoured by a hungry night.

I celebrate the light of Superior on film. Light saturates in spring and the landscape is immersed in green hues. The early morning whistle of white-throated sparrows begins well before dawn. Then sunlight becomes greedy. Near the summer solstice, the nights are brief. But summers soon fade. Days shrink. Shadows grow. A brief autumn palette is quickly swept away by the brisk winds of an anxious winter. In this harshest of seasons, the sun strikes a minor arc along the southern horizon. Light becomes a precious commodity. Yet, when sunbeams slice through overcast skies, they brilliantly illuminate. Trees and boulders are dwarfed by their own ominous shadows.

The qualities of light change with the moment, the hour, the day, and month. A fog lifts. Clouds gather. A frequently visited location lures me back in other seasons or times of day simply because I know the conditions will dress it differently. I shoot with urgency knowing the cobblestone beach, jagged cliff, or birch grove will never look the same again. But I hesitate because the image might be better if I'm patient. The light's angle and colors will play with the ornate surfaces of nature in new ways in an hour or tomorrow. Each scene is reinvented by its illumination. In an instant, the moment is lost as a new scene is born.

Light is dynamic. I venture into the darkness to catch the dawn. I linger until last light, capturing wonder before it fades. Film is my canvas. Light is my paint.

The feathery
silhouettes of
jack pines appear
softer when encased
in morning fog.
Pictured Rocks
National Lakeshore

Union Bay's shoreline
is glazed with burnt
orange reflections on
this spring morning.
Porcupine Mountains
Wilderness State Park

Raking light emphasizes the highly weathered volcanic rock along the coastal trail in Ashburton Bay. Neys Provincial Park

Golden light gilds the surface of Little Sand Bay on
a summer evening. Apostle Islands National Lakeshore

Overleaf:
The ancient, wrinkled cliffs overlooking Old Woman Bay are hidden
beneath an icy cape illuminated at sunset. Lake Superior Provincial Park

Warm only to the eye, sunlight provides little comfort to Shovel Point on this bitter morning. Tettegouche State Park

Clouds and water are separated by a wedge of light along Esrey Point in the Keweenaw Peninsula.

A pink sun drips from a periwinkle sky before settling on the edge of night.
Twelve Mile Beach, Pictured Rocks National Lakeshore

Behind a frozen
waterfall, hanging
crystals create an
ethereal world bathed
in glowing green.
Pictured Rocks
National Lakeshore

Summer glistens on peaceful waters in Oiseau Bay. Pukaskwa National Park

A quiet cove of shallow water encourages a dancing web of spectral light on York Island. Apostle Islands National Lakeshore

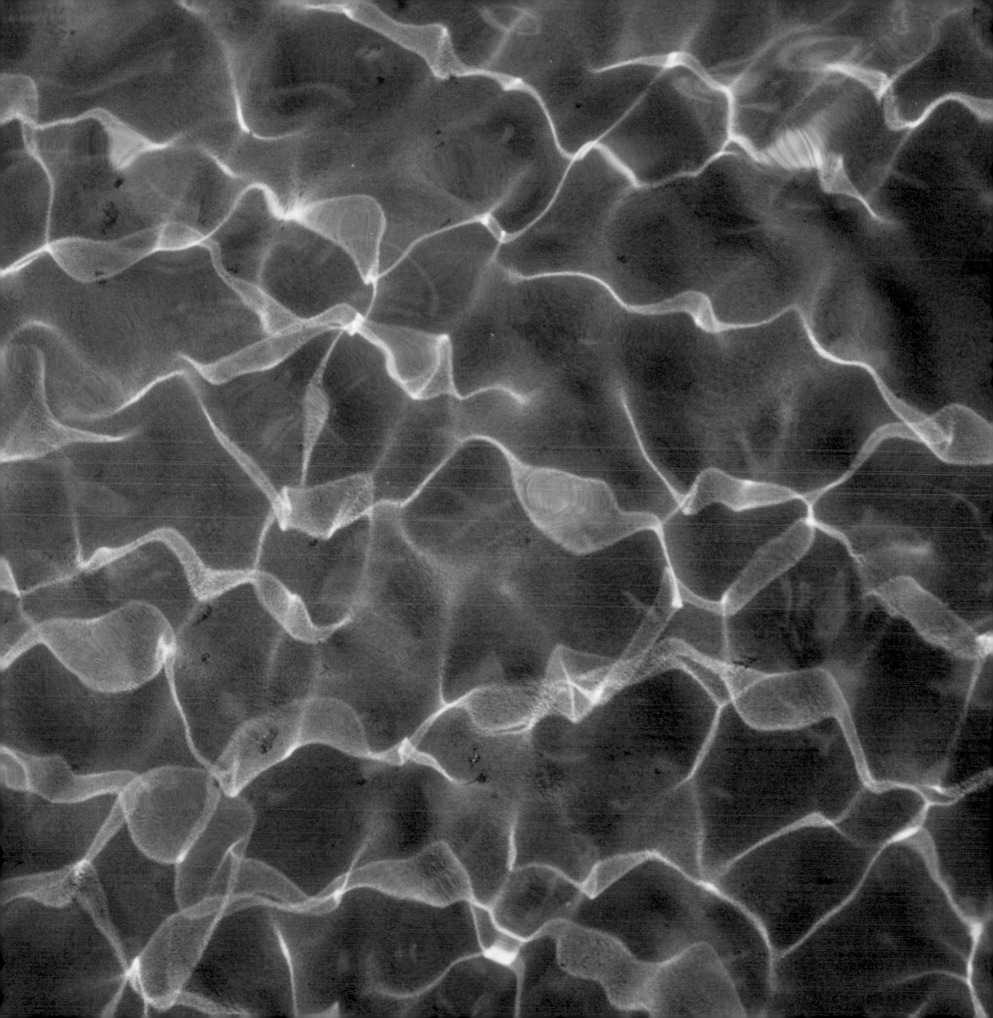

Superior is renowned for storm-driven waves, but on this evening, the moon finds calm waters on Whitefish Bay.

Overleaf:
Lit by a setting early August sun, hidden secrets await discovery in a deep cave chamber.
Apostle Islands National Lakeshore

Horizontal light accentuates the yellow-green of aspens in late spring. Sleeping Giant Provincial Park

While this bog of tall spruce is often frequented by moose, the only visitor this autumn morning is frost. Lake Superior Provincial Park

A lonely winter scene
along Little Sand Bay
echoes a distant
arctic landscape.
Apostle Islands
National Lakeshore

Impressionistic reflections of autumn shimmer
in Thornton Lake. Hiawatha National Forest

Massive boulders lie buried in a cold teal graveyard illuminated
by soft morning sunlight. Gooseberry Falls State Park

Dark shadows melt as daylight creeps into the hidden corners of Moskey Basin. Isle Royale National Park

A rolling cascade captures morning light near the mouth of the Presque Isle River. Porcupine Mountains Wilderness State Park

Light through late afternoon storm clouds highlight gentle waves lapping at the shore of West Caribou Island. Isle Royale National Park

Overleaf: With more than three hundred miles to the distant shore, these late September clouds have room to roam. Cascade River State Park

Slowly drifting clouds are left to wander in darkness as the sun sinks behind Grand Island, Michigan.

Whispers may be shy and elusive. Others are loud and exposed like this lichen-dappled boulder on a beach of naked cobblestones. Old Woman Bay, Lake Superior Provincial Park

Why does one expanse of granite catch my eye? Is it the flitting of the warbler in the brush or its almost inaudible call that draws me to it? What is it about the tattered bark on one birch that speaks to me in a grove of many? The grandeur of Lake Superior fills one's vision on the first visit. It bowls one over. But once you become acclimated to its scale, it is the whispers from nature that provide enduring intrigue.

Forget your schedule. Nature's stories are told at an unhurried pace. Attune all of your senses. Listen. Do you hear faint, unfamiliar sounds? Discover the colors and patterns around you. Stand still. Watch the dune grass respond to the wind. Close your eyes. Smell the scent of spruce weaving through the mist from breaking waves. Wait. The whispers come when you allow them time to unfold. Follow the flight of the gull as it lands on the beach. Watch as it takes wing again to surf on rolling waves of wind over the lake.

On one Indian summer day near the mouth of the Presque Isle River, a soft breeze sighed through the ancient pine boughs overhead. I watched as birds and insects whirled through the air. A lull in the breeze turned my attention to a trickling in the river below my cliffside perch. Tiny foam bubbles floated past me in cirrus-like formations. An occasional birch or maple leaf joined the parade to give it color and cadence. It was visual, fluid music. On that day, it resonated within me. On the next, I may have missed it.

The haunting call of a loon. The bittersweet taste of wild blueberries. The teasing touch of a warm February breeze. Fog lifting as dawn breaks. While they may be faint and fleeting, the richness of the region is revealed when we catch the whispers.

Multicolored cobblestones slowly emerge from continually shifting sands along the Old Woman River. Lake Superior Provincial Park

Deep maroon draws attention to the tiny rose-like cones on boughs of feathery tamarack needles.

Dune grasses sway with summer breezes as a
soft sun descends to the horizon in Au Train Bay.

On a winter morning, a hoar frost garden blooms in the
frigid sand. Horseshoe Bay, Pukaskwa National Park

A gentle evening wave sweeps onto Twelve Mile Beach erasing a jumble of gull tracks.
Pictured Rocks National Lakeshore

In temperatures of twenty-five below zero, a red squirrel
takes a moment during seed collecting to warm his paws.

Overleaf:
Birch leaves and bubbles drift lazily by on a balmy autumn afternoon.
Presque Isle River, Porcupine Mountains Wilderness State Park

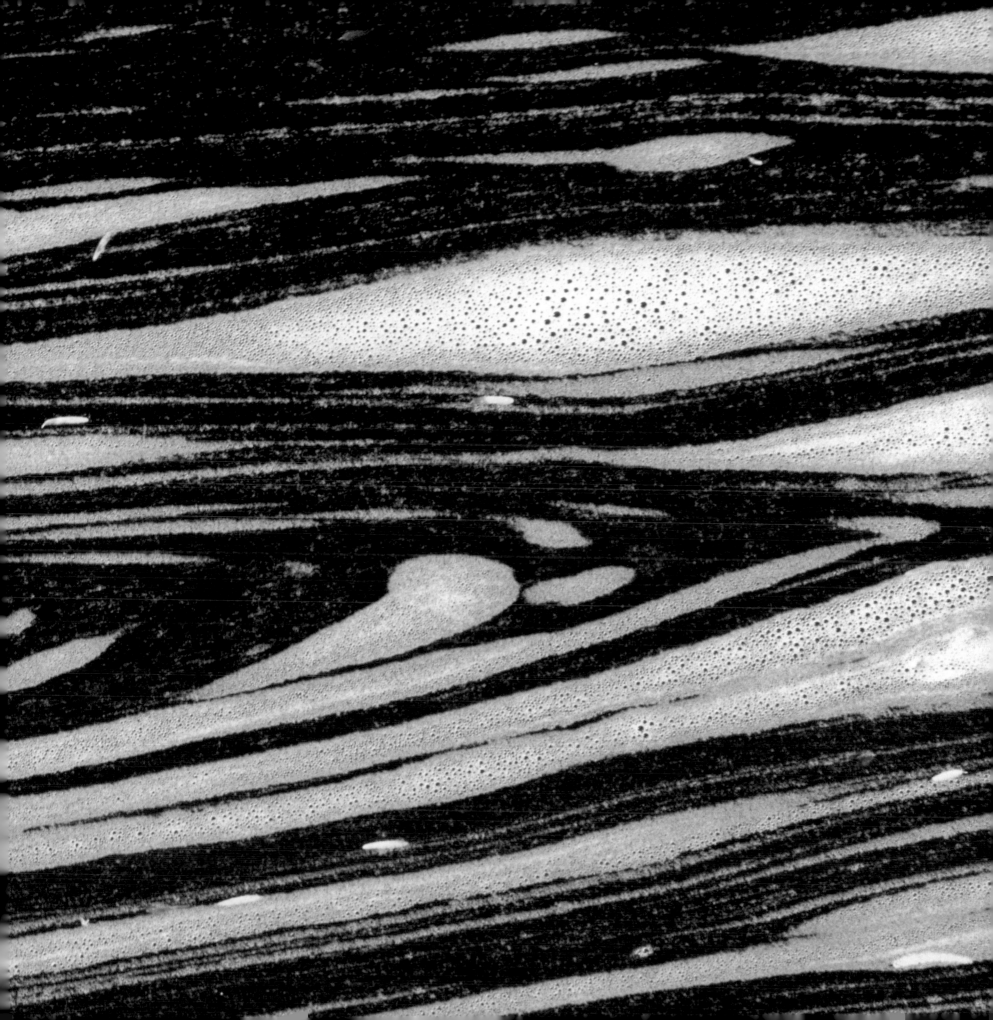

Organic patterns are
embossed in the sand
by a trickling stream.
Pictured Rocks
National Lakeshore

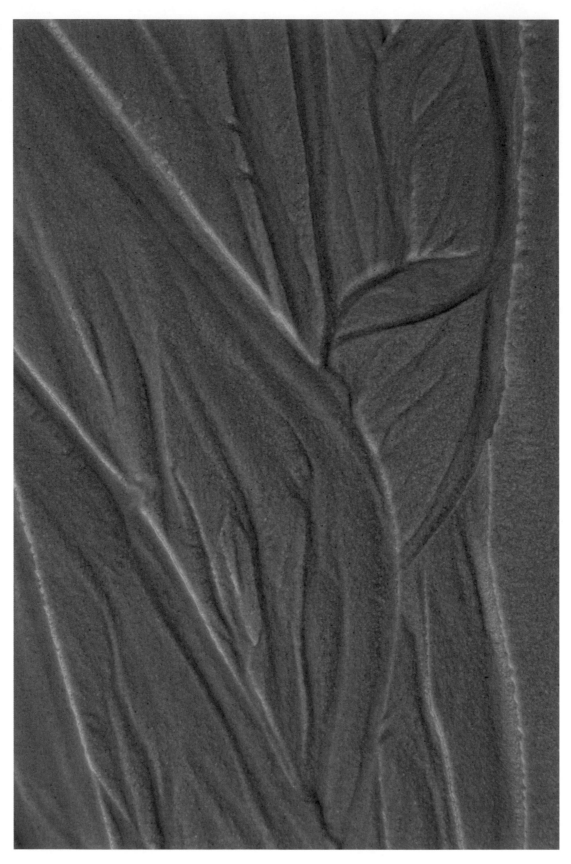

Lime and magenta swirl through a lush carpet of sphagnum moss in the dark,
damp boreal forest around Rustle Lake. Lake Superior Provincial Park

The essence of birch trees is found in the diverse textures of their delicate skin. Strips of bark litter the snow after a winter storm in Obatanga Provincial Park.

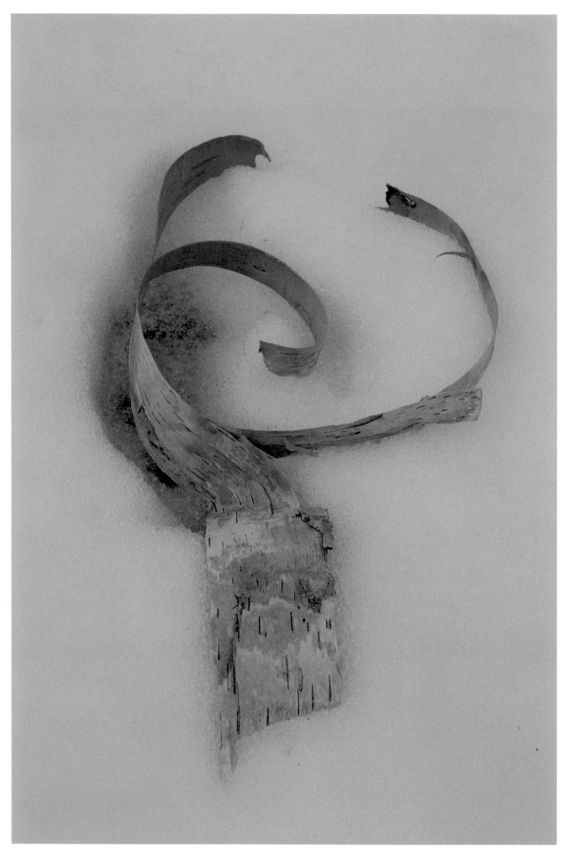

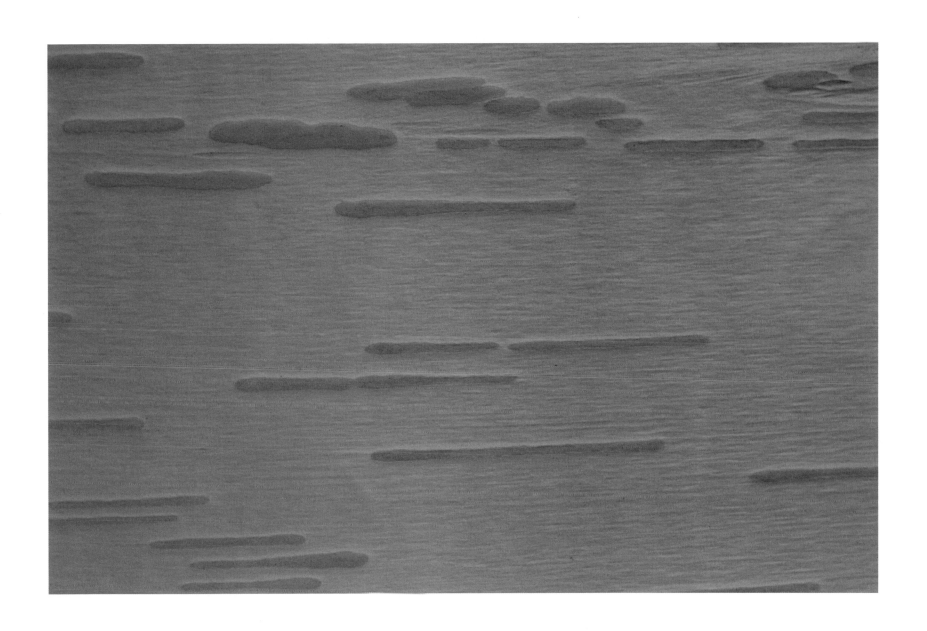

Beneath the chalky white exterior, birch trees are wrapped in smooth warm tones.

Granite is a tapestry of earthly pastels in
Simons Harbour. Pukaskwa National Park

A boulder encrusted with lichen finds refuge in golden grasses
on a cold and barren coast. Gooseberry Falls State Park

In a sanctuary of decaying leaves, Indian pipe flowers congregate and bow their heads in silence.

Spring arrives in celebration as buds dress in their finest costumes while a Wilson's warbler sings.

Having traveled from unknown shores, these grand nomads find their final resting place on a rocky promontory. Pukaskwa National Park

*T*he horseshoe-shaped beach lay hidden beneath a web of logs. Massive trunks of birch, maple, pine, and spruce lay like interwoven fingers. From what distant shores had these grand nomads come? What tossed them like kindling on this beach?

Powerful natural forces put the bedrock and living things at risk here. Throughout the seasons, the combined strength of the wind and water rules this region with wild mood swings. When enraged, cobblestones tumble into pebbles. Thick sheets of ice drive into jagged piles that linger on beaches. Blinding snowstorms bury the land. It may be the middle of June before delicate tree buds emerge. When placid, pebbles gently churn into sand. July breezes pollinate wildflowers. Eagles dance on spiraling currents.

Enigmatic power exists here as well. The lake inspires and soothes. As mist from the whitecaps settled on the sands of Old Woman Bay, the lake roared. An earth-toned woman with straight, dark hair approached the crashing waves. With eyes toward the lake, she reached into a fringed leather satchel. Stretching her arms out in the sun, she stood in silent meditation communing with the lake. She bent to lay a pinch of tobacco gently in the wet sand and remained for another contemplative moment. Turning toward the land, she caught sight of me. Nodding, she smiled and left without a word.

Superior has an imposing presence. While its dense fogs and lake-effect snows creep past its shores, the lake's spirit extends far beyond its realm. It ignites our imagination. That is its most essential power.

A forest of birches
slowly drown in a
sea of wind-driven
sand behind the
Grand Sable Dunes.
Pictured Rocks
National Lakeshore

Autumn birch leaves steal a ride to shore on rolling waves along Sand Point. Pictured Rocks National Lakeshore

Overleaf:
A virgin eastern hemlock forest provides a glimpse into history. Trappers, voyageurs, and traders wandered past their massive trunks. Porcupine Mountains Wilderness State Park

The islands along the unforgiving coast of Pukaskwa National Park are splashed with a medley of colored lichens. In Pulpwood Harbour, yellow-greens dominate.

Rusty orange lichens
prevail on stark
islands at the north
entrance to scenic
Oiseau Bay.

Ornate bowls reveal the powerful nature of water when it is combined with time and movement.
Presque Isle River, Porcupine Mountains Wilderness State Park

Gossamer sheets
heave skyward as
Superior breaks free
from its icy sheath
near Hattie Cove.
Pukaskwa
National Park

Tannin-tinged water carves many paths as it
thunders over High Falls. Grand Portage State Park

Waves uncover a treasure trove of
visual riches at Muskallonge State Park.

Enriched with petroglyphs, Agawa Rock is a place of mystery and spirit. For centuries, offerings have been left at this site to ensure safe travel on unpredictable waters. Lake Superior Provincial Park

A lone birch tree
selects a sandstone
home complete
with a sunset view.
Apostle Islands
National Lakeshore

Once flowing with liquid earth, solidified veins
now snake through the primordial coastline in
Robertson Cove. Lake Superior Provincial Park

*T*ales written in the snow by untamed authors criss-cross the wintery landscape. I discovered one of these stories while snowshoeing around Rustle Lake. My trek through the cedars brought me to icy moose tracks. They joined the trail from my left. Further along, wolf tracks merged from the right. The unseen travelers' synchronized footprints followed the trail for several hundred yards. Abruptly, the prints moved through snow too deep to follow. Did these two wanderers meet on their journeys? Who set the pace, the pursued or the pursuer?

Past and present stories of the region lie scattered across this unyielding landscape. Some are lengthy novels. Others read like poems. Nature's ghostwriters flourish here as residents and transients. Geologic events and weather write as eloquently as plants, mammals, and birds.

This granite journal also contains human memoirs. Only the shells of crumbling buildings remain. The voices are silent. The copper is gone. Walking through the mine ruins, I sensed the only urgency here was spring's rush to banish a winter reluctant to leave. Signs of the once bustling community surrounded me along with the presence of other forces. Decades of wind, freezing, and thawing have chiseled the mortar holding stone walls together. Once powerful machinery now lies dormant under a gnarled skin of rust. Eventually, the walls will fade into the hillside. Nature prevails as birches reclaim their homeland inside the roofless foundry. In time, the only voices heard will be the birch family conversing with the wind.

Superior's waves quickly erase my footprints in the wet sand. The hand hewn beam, the painted rock wall, the lightning-charred stump, and the beaver lodge will all eventually vanish. Nature returns to its true state in time. Everything passing through here leaves its trace for only a moment, a season, an eon or two. These traces weave a rich tapestry of true and imagined stories.

Along the Big Iron River, blush-colored finger paintings adorn a gray canvas. The next day, light rains washed away the river otter's art.

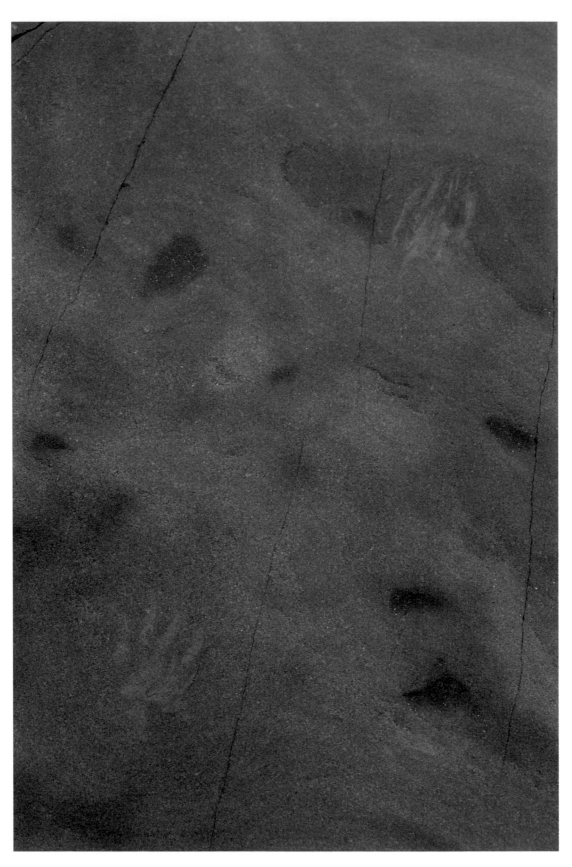

A family of birches takes up residence in the ruins of the Delaware Copper Mine on the Keweenaw Peninsula.

A spruce tree now grows where men once sat. In the 1940s, this old boat transported prisoners of war up the Little Pic River to chop down trees in the logging camps. Neys Provincial Park

Mysterious cobblestone structures left by ancient people dot the untamed shores of Pukaskwa National Park. Were they used for vision quests, as hunting blinds or shelters? Some secrets are kept by the lake.

Overleaf:
In the form of massive sandstone arches along Squaw Bay, waves and weather have carved their footprints. Apostle Islands National Lakeshore

Ancient stories are written in red ochre on stone cliffs at Agawa Rock. Lake Superior Provincial Park

A wooden picket fence and gravestone are painted emerald with lichen on Cemetery Island. Isle Royale National Park

Waves from passing summer storms deposit pebbles in a carved depression along the shore. Tettegouche State Park

A shipwreck slowly
decomposing in
the surf gathers
cobblestones in
its skeletal remains
at Au Sable Point.
Pictured Rocks
National Lakeshore

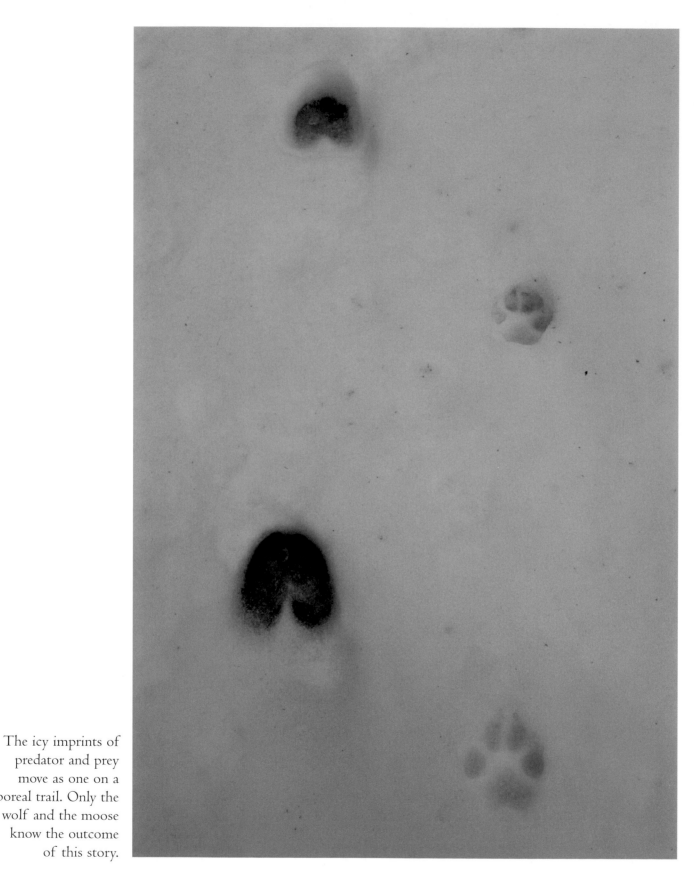

Freshly chewed branches are a sign that a beaver family occupies this weathered lodge.

The icy imprints of predator and prey move as one on a boreal trail. Only the wolf and the moose know the outcome of this story.

Pukaskwa's granite coast, left scarred by mile-thick glaciers, now warms under a summer sunset.

A huge erratic escaped from its moving tomb of glacial ice only to be
imprisoned again by a steadfast white pine. Lake Superior Provincial Park

Evening sunlight warms an ancient
wave of sandstone near Miner's Beach.
Pictured Rocks National Lakeshore

Dramatic events fill this wild stage. Overtures may lead to impressive grand finales or minor individual performances. The audiences along these shores, however, must have patience and be attuned to nature's nuances.

Bird songs dwindled and the day's warmth drifted away. Oscillating on the northern horizon was a faint green shimmer. Then stars grew bright against the curtain of black. Sleep would have to wait as the northern lights moved to center stage.

Celestial phantoms robed in glowing red and green gowns danced above the Earth. The light was an energized breeze. By midnight, it was as bright as dawn. It provoked the birds to assemble a mixed chorus. Loons wailed. White-throated sparrows whistled. An American bittern kerplunked in the nearby marsh. Late into the night, distant thumps from a drumming ruffed grouse lulled me to sleep. But far too early, morning chased away the night sky and the secret nocturnal celebration.

On another stage during another performance, the twitch of an ear directed my eyes to a curious wolf on the far shore of Moskey Basin. Acting as narrator, he turned his head over his shoulder then exited through the curtain of spruce behind him. Without warning, a cow moose splashed into knee-deep water. Behind her, in rapid pursuit, a bull entered with an impressive set of antlers. The cow dashed to shore and fled into the woods with the suitor gaining on her. Grunting, he crashed into the forest oblivious to the trees in his path. Branches snapped. Leaves flew. Quickly, the commotion faded as they charged into thick underbrush.

The earth rumbles along raging streams. Territorial battles erupt. Sudden storms develop. Springs burst forth. Autumn colors explode. Wings swoop at wary prey. This lavish Lake Superior saga, containing eons of dramatic scenes, is still being created within its northern wilderness theatre.

The northern lights spill from the Big Dipper into Union Bay. Porcupine Mountains Wilderness State Park

After a long leap over the lake, the sun finally settles between two islands in Sinclair Cove. Lake Superior Provincial Park

A two-week-old common loon chick dozes one quiet summer morning on its downy waterbed.

Where the sugar maple reaches its northern limits, the grand finale of autumn is made more dramatic by the presence of evergreens. Lake Superior Provincial Park

An early October snow squall off the coast reminds us that winter
can come ahead of schedule in this region. Copper Harbor, Michigan

Miner's Castle looms high over Superior set ablaze by a fiery sunset.
Pictured Rocks National Lakeshore

Throughout the
Lake Superior region,
marsh marigolds are
a harbinger of spring

Two-story-high crystals hang like stalactites from the Squaw Bay caves. Apostle Islands National Lakeshore

Light and wind dance at dawn. Palisade Head, Tettegouche State Park

A snowshoe hare becomes a magician and disappears into a world of white mounds along Lake Superior.

Silent as falling snow, a lynx glides through a boreal forest in search of unlucky prey.

Cold, snow, and wind conspire to create a lunar landscape on Perry Bay. Sleeping Giant Provincial Park

Sunrise ignites a wildfire in the clouds above a lonely maple tree near Marquette, Michigan.

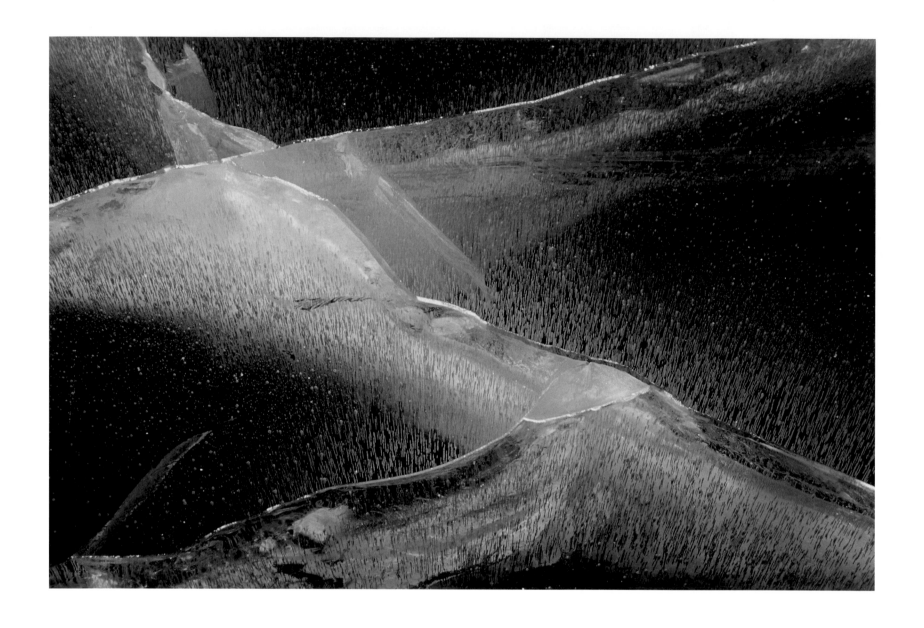

Deep rumbles reverberate as thick ice fractures. It is evidence of the clash raging between
Superior and the unrelenting winter. Finlay Bay, Sleeping Giant Provincial Park

Patience is rewarded when pink and indigo paint the landscape after sunset.
Michipicoten Post Provincial Park

As a storm front retreats over Old Woman Bay, the sun slips in and out of the clouds while racing toward the horizon. Lake Superior Provincial Park

A male ruffed grouse displays his blue-edged mane to impress
a female feeding on birch catkins in the branches above him.

Turbulent clouds rushing southward along the coast of Tettegouche State Park are pierced by a sliver of light.

This glowing sandstone sentinel guards the entrance to the
Squaw Bay caves at dusk. Apostle Islands National Lakeshore

Overleaf:
The continuous thunder from this liquid staircase
fills the ancient pine forest above the Presque Isle
River. Porcupine Mountains Wilderness State Park

Terraced sandstone glows at the
end of the day at Miner's Beach.
Pictured Rocks National Lakeshore

I stand once again on this grand shore.
The crisp blue horizon fills my field of vision and imagination. Lake Superior has dominated
my photography for many years. I have sought its spirit and surrendered to it.
I have admired its majesty and pursued its secrets.

The stoic rhythms of this wild place have transformed me
as a man and photographer. I learned about light here. I developed an appreciation for subtle color
and form. These shores have honed my skills in observation and patience. By deeply exploring the region,
I discovered the significance of all untamed places.

A coyote's yelp harmonizing with a prairie sunset.
Endless horizons seen from atop a tundra ridge. A campfire's hypnotic effect. The jolt brought by fresh
grizzly tracks found on the trail. Anywhere we touch nature, we are touched in return. We realize we are
part of the landscape, not the center of it, and we are humbled. As each of us experiences the
natural world, our primal core is nourished. It comforts our soul.

While many journeys have a final destination, this one does not.
The secrets still kept by the Lake will continue to lure me back. I will delve deeper into the region's
unique spirit to reach its intangible heart.

LAKE SUPERIOR REGION

ONTARIO
1 Batchawana Bay Provincial Park
2 Pancake Bay Provincial Park
3 Lake Superior Provincial Park
4 Michipicoten Post Provincial Park
5 Michipicoten Island Provincial Park
6 Obatanga Provincial Park
7 White Lake Provincial Park
8 Pukaskwa National Park
9 Neys Provincial Park
10 Slate Islands Provincial Park
11 Rainbow Falls Provincial Park
12 Ouimet Canyon Provincial Park
13 Sleeping Giant Provincial Park

MINNESOTA
14 Grand Portage State Park
15 Grand Portage National Monument
16 Judge C. R. Magney State Park
17 Cascade River State Park
18 Superior National Forest
19 Temperance River State Park
20 George Crosby Manitou State Park
21 Tettegouche State Park
22 Split Rock Lighthouse State Park
23 Gooseberry Falls State Park

WISCONSIN
24 Apostle Islands National Lakeshore
25 Chequamegon National Forest

MICHIGAN
26 Isle Royale National Park
27 Porcupine Mountains Wilderness State Park
28 Keweenaw Peninsula
29 Ottawa National Forest
30 Huron Islands National Wildlife Refuge
31 Hiawatha National Forest
32 Pictured Rocks National Lakeshore
33 Muskallonge Lake State Park
34 Whitefish Point
35 Tahquamenon Falls State Park

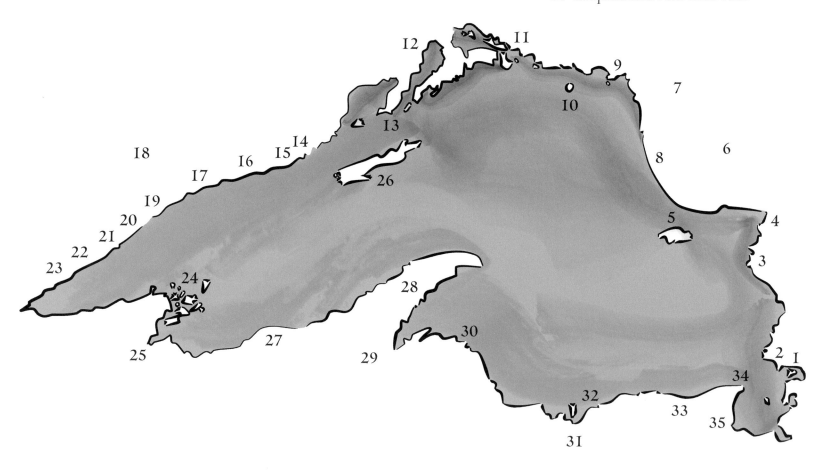